Anna Maria Wormald de Blaquière

Pilgrims

A Poem

Anna Maria Wormald de Blaquière

Pilgrims
A Poem

ISBN/EAN: 9783337293826

Printed in Europe, USA, Canada, Australia, Japan

Cover: Foto ©Thomas Meinert / pixelio.de

More available books at **www.hansebooks.com**

PILGRIMS:

A Poem.

BY THE

HON. MRS. DE BLAQUIÈRE.

———◆———

PRIVATELY PRINTED.

1869.

THIS LITTLE WORK IS

DEDICATED

TO

𝔐𝔶 𝔇𝔢𝔞𝔯 𝔐𝔬𝔱𝔥𝔢𝔯,

TO WHOSE KIND ENCOURAGEMENT

ITS COMPLETION IS

MAINLY DUE.

PILGRIMS.

Life's Pilgrims! struggling to attain some shrine
Of faith, love, liberty, or whate'er truth,
Or small, or great, the soul has strength to grasp
By which to raise itself from earth to Heaven.
Unsatisfied—in that the end is seen
Not *here* but *there.*

I.

Near where the Tiber's patriarchal flow
Rolls 'neath the arches of the Angelo,
A palace stands.
                    In vain the lucent smile
Of sunshine lingers on the gloomy pile ;
No sun however bright can e'er restore
The glories Time has dimmed for evermore !
Above the portals, half defaced by age,
Some sculptured arms bespeak a lineage
Princely and old.   A warrior of the line,
In the Crusades of Holy Palestine,

Had chosen in remembrance of the war
For badge, a crescent and attendant star,
With motto circling ; " From the Eastern sky
I shall return in greater majesty."
Vain words ! which now a ruined shield infold
To mock the glories that they once foretold.

Beyond the entrance is a court inlaid
With marbles, girded by a wide arcade,
'Neath which amidst the solemn shadows lie
Fragments of torsi and sarcophagi,
Within Campagna's mighty storehouse found—
For countless ages buried underground.
But where the court is open to the day,
Half shrouded in a fountain's glistening spray,
Is crouched the Queen of Love, whilst from her
          shell
The plaintive waters murmuring to the well,
Appear lamenting with soft falling tears,
The pow'r and glory of departed years.

Around the Court, within th' encircling walls,
Are ranged saloons and mirth-chilled banquet
          halls,

Where not an echo lingers to recall
The revels of forgotten festival.
Adorned are they by master-hands of yore
With frescoed scenes of legendary lore ;
Or hung with treasures from the Flemish looms,
Which, dimly seen within the darkened rooms,
Suspend in epic folds upon the wall—
Of their own splendour, the funereal pall !
Sometimes it chances that an errant ray
Creeps in, and glides across the tapestry,
As though t'would fain restore with gleaming
    thread
The lustre other suns have witherèd.
'Tis then, perchance—deserting worlds above—
That round the arras the dead craftsmen move,
Who, faithful still to work they loved of old,
Repair their weaving with celestial gold.
Within the galleries—in state enshrined—
Repose the relics of creative mind.
There, on the canvas, lastingly endure
The mellow tints of Titian of Cadore ;
And fervidly th' unrivalled colours glow
Of Castel Franco's wondrous Georgio,

Whilst saintly figures rest beneath the spell
Of Urbino's inspired Raphael.
These gems of art their serried ranks maintain,
Though wealth and influential grandeur wane ;
For fallen nobles guard with jealous pride
Those heirlooms that the Past has sanctified,
Preserving still th' illusory display
Of dignity, when power has passed away,
And idly bask within the slanting rays
Of glory lingering from the former days.
But some there are with loftier dreams of
    fame,
Who scorn the borrowed halo of a Name,
Save as a basis to be fraught anew
With the great actions they themselves shall do.
'Tis thus that Claudio, of th' illustrious line
Descending from the Knight of Palestine,
Has learned to estimate his lineage,
And prize his now impoverished heritage,
As workmen glory in the fallen tree
For which they shape a nobler destiny.
No charm for him possess the pictured walls,
The phantom honour of his fathers' halls ;

No charm for him the false inglorious pride
That lingers vainly where all else has died ;
Undazzled by his predecessors' state,
Their acts alone he yearns to emulate.
His mind already plans heroic schemes—
And—not content with ineffectual dreams—
He is enrolled within the patriot band
Of heroes vowed to die, or free their land.

  *   *   *   *   *

It is the eve of Lent.
      Avoiding all
The crowds assembled for the Carnival,
Claudio the Ghetto treads.   No tinted ray
Can enter there to charm the night away
Or woo one instant from the darkness.   Where
The shadows cluster in the Cenci Square
He passes—heedless of Beatrice's fate,
And through the archway of the Jewish Gate
Speeds to the Quattro Capi,* where the skies
Are flooded with the day's last brilliancies,

---

* The Bridge of Quattro Capi is the ancient Pons Fabricius. It crosses the Tiber to the Island of Æsculapius, or Isola di San Bartolomeo. The piers of the arches are ornamented with heads of Janus.

Whilst—as unto a sacrificial fire—
Phœbus sinks slowly to the funeral pyre
Himself has kindled.   With a last caress
He bathes the world he leaves in loveliness,
And his extended arms of flame infold
Trastevere's* proud walls, and change to gold
The sepia palaces.

　　　　　　Upon the piers,
Which Janus guards throughout the changing
　　　years,
The radiance strikes and casts upon the tide,
Their forms reflected quivering side by side.
Ah! would that Truth and Liberty had given
Their light where only now shines that of
　　　Heaven!
Borne from afar the giddy Maskers' cries,
Strike dissonant with Roman destinies.

"Unseemly jesters! Romans but in name!
Can ye thus wantonly parade your shame,

---

* The inhabitants of Trastevere claim the purest Roman
descent; and, it is said, refuse to intermarry with their fellow
citizens on the opposite bank of the Tiber.

Letting your tyrants triumph as they see
How they have crushed your last of dignity?
Yet thanks to heaven! some few remain to us
Who dwell in Rome and yet are valorous!
Some few chivalrous hearts who soon shall hold
No broken mirror to the days of old!"

Thus Claudio—then whilst in the fading west,
The last long sunbeam folds itself to rest,
And all the beauties of the wearied light
Sink softly sleeping to the arms of night,
He passes on unto that island shore
Whence Æsculapius in the days of yore,
Transported from the distant shrines of Greece
In serpent semblance, made the plague to
    cease.
There—from a vault-like entry, high and wide,
Chilled by the vapours from the neighbouring
    tide,—
A lantern swings. Beneath its flickering glare
Arise the marbles of a time-worn stair,
Up which springs Claudio to a spacious room
Where age has settled moodily to gloom,

Where tattered curtains brown with time and
  dust
And arms once red with blood, but now with
  rust,
And faded frescoes of that marriage day*
Centaurs dishonoured by a murderous fray—
Are all commingled in a misty haze,
Within a shaded lamp's uncertain rays.

A restless figure pacing to and fro
Starts with a greeting;
                    "Welcome, Claudio!
Again are we the first!
                    These schemes allay
The thirst for right that rots my life away!
There is a burning zeal within my soul
Impatient of the maddening control
Delay exacts, and which would rashly break
All barriers of prudence, and would make
This revolution by one mighty blow!
By one fell swoop sink all our tyrants low!"

---

* Marriage day of Pirithous.

" Yet is there sometimes reason in delay
For actions too precipitant might stay
The cause they blindly purpose to progress
And stem the chance of ultimate success."

And then, as rebel stars meet one by one
To claim the empire of the setting sun,
Come other patriots to discuss the schemes
By which they hope to realize their dreams ;
And Claudio, rising to address the band,
Accents his words with an uplifted hand :

" As when some warrior overcome by pain
And long unconscious on the bloody plain,
Revives, to aim an unexpected blow
With deadly vigour at his heedless foe,—
E'en thus the spirit of the Roman race,
Subdued, enfeebled, conquered for a space,
Revives, with subtle purpose to oppose
Th' ascendency of Rome's triumphant foes !
Unhappy Rome ! where truth has lost her
        light,
And wrong bewilders in the garb of right.

Oh ! men of Rome ! sons of a race of kings !
Whose valour, echoing through the ages,
    rings
Like martial music from a distant plain
Resounding midst the mountains,—now again
Renew the strain, that it may never die,
But vibrate onward to eternity !"
He pauses,—for a whisper smites his ear :
" Hist ! speak no further — there's a traitor
    here !"

As when some startled gazer's heav'n-turned
    glance
Beholds a meteor flash the dark expanse,
And striving to discern its course afar,
Deems each unchanging orb the fallen star,—
E'en thus do Claudio's troubled glances fall
On those around—suspicious of them all !
Unconsciously he grasps the ready knife—
The prompt defender of the Roman's life.

" Nay, stay thy weapon, noble Claudio ; wait—
All may be lost if too precipitate.

See where yon tapestries so darkly fall
Beside that frescoed panel in the wall,
There stand three figures—two of them we know,
The Counts of Benvicin' and Urbino,—
The third—who with such obvious caution holds
Himself enveloped in his toga's folds—
Say, know'st thou him ?"

               " No ! but per Bacco ! soon
Too well for him I'll know the base poltroon !"
And shaking off his friend's restraining clasp,
He springs upon the foe !   With iron grasp
He brands his strength upon the muffled arm,
Whilst through th' assembly spreads a vague
    alarm,
And shouts commingle in a deafening cry,
"A spy ! secure the traitor ! treachery !"
Then midst the clamour, rising sweet and clear
A voice is heard, " Unhand me, Prince !   For-
    bear !"

Unmanned and vanquished by a single word,
Claudio starts back dismayed !   His hand has
    stirred

The toga's folds—they fall—and tumult dies
Before the radiance of a woman's eyes !
A woman ! Of that beauteous type which smiles
Upon Venetia's Venus favoured isles !
As bright the shimmering of her golden hair
As though the Lido's sands were sprinkled
     there ;
As deep the lustre of her purple eyes
As moonlit ether in Italian skies.
Half shrouded by an emerald-gleaming vest,
Emotion troubled heaves her snowy breast,
Arising purely from the folds beneath
As a white flow'ret from its verdant sheath.

" Melina !—Here !—at night !—alone ! " Thus
     low,
In broken utterances, Claudio.

" Nay, chide me not ; an over-acted jest
Has brought me hither,—an unwelcome guest."

Thus she—soft-toned—to him, and then aloud,
With words submissive, but with gesture proud—

As of a queen dethronèd, who would hide
Her loss of dignity by added pride—
" Romans ! the plea I offer to you all
Must be the licence of the Carnival.
My cousin Claudio, importunèd long,
Refused to join the Corso's brilliant throng,
And half in wonder, half in girlish glee,
I vowed to solve th' unwonted mystery
Of his ascetic mood ; and, unbetrayed
Beneath this toga's friendly folds, I strayed,
Pursuing him across the Tiber's flood,
And thus—beyond the bounds of maidenhood.
And now *my* honour rests with *you*, whilst *I*
Hold secrets hazarding *your* liberty ;
In mutual threats then, be our safety laid,
Who first denounces, be at once betrayed !"

She pauses, and as music from a song
Suspended, on the hushed air vibrates long,
E'en thus her accents thrill throughout the
    hall,
Nor die till they have touched the hearts of
    all.

And then the Leader of the rebel band
With reverence kneels to kiss the lady's hand;
" Believe us, Princess, we would rather see
Our visions fade like golden mists at sea,
And forfeit all our glorious dreams by death,
Than wrong thy virtue by a single breath;
Not all the laurels from the brow of Fame
Absolve the slanderer of a woman's name!"

And Claudio, silent whilst his leader speaks,
Marks well the haughty glance and kindling
        cheeks
Of her, whose beauteousness seems made to try
How swift from heav'n love's wingèd darts can
        fly!
Yet in his breast forebodings strange and dim
Annul the magic of her charms for him.

Thus sometimes when the northern ocean
        gleams
Exultant in the summer's radiant beams,
A breath from unseen ice-realms chills the air,
Prognostic of the spectres lurking there.

Then quietly from where its folds have lain
Lifting the fallen mantle, and again
Shrouding her with it from betraying sight,
He leads Melina out into the night.
The night! so solemn—so intensely still,
That silence—void of earth-sounds—seems to fill
With spiritual whisperings, that may
Be echoes from the bright worlds far away.
Then on his ear a murmur like a charm
Falls softly, whilst a hand entwines his arm.

" My Claudio, cousin, why so stern—so grave ?
It was not thus the ancient Roman brave
Responded to the presence of the fair,
Nor left unstruck the chords of moonlit air ! "

He answers mournfully ;
                      " 'Twere best to leave
The chords   untouched,   than   tune   them   to
        deceive,
And   did   I   speak   my   thoughts,   my   words
        would be
Not such, perchance, as thou would'st hear."

Then she ;
" Say what thou wilt. I know men deem me
    proud—
But see yon moon, emerging from a cloud,
Unchangeable and cold to every sun,
Except her only loved peculiar one,—
Thus, friend of childhood, art thou all to me,
My heart, if cold to others, warms to thee !
Then fear not that my haughtiness repel
The confidence of one I love—*too well !*"

Confounded in one long impassioned sigh,
The last two words, unheard, unvalued, die !

" My thoughts," he answers, " tremble in my
    breast,
Like frightened birds that dare not pause to rest,
Nor stay to let us count th' intricate rings
Of changing colour in their agile wings.
Thoughts of those now irrevocable hours,
When all thy charms, like partly opened flowers,
Reserved their beauty for the only eye
That stooped to mark their early brilliancy.

But now, alas ! in these less happy days
Th' expanded blossoms court each idler's gaze,
And lose their sweetness in the heart of one
Who values only what is his alone.
Thou say'st men deem thee proud,—'tis true,—
    and yet
'Twas a strange pride that led thee to forget,
As on this night, that woman's surest tie
Upon a man's true love is modesty !
Pride—born of vanity !—that condescends
To court the very notice that offends ! ''

He pauses—for within his listener's eyes
The liquid fires of indignation rise,
And darkening their pathway shadows fall,
Dropped at the foot of a palatial wall.
'' My home !'' Melina cries, '' Alas ! that I
From *thy* reproach should need its sanctuary !''
Then from his side swift springs the angered
    maid,
Lost in a moon-twined labyrinth of shade.

C

II.

" What mystic awe th' enthusiast's bosom fills
Before the City of the Seven Hills !
The mausoleum of a race of kings !
Amidst the walls the creeping ivy clings,
Binding the mouldering clay and crumbling
       stones
With martyrs' ashes and with emperors' bones !
Behold her now, as mournfully she lies
Beneath the radiance of the Southern skies,
For faithful nature does not change with fate,
And even smiles upon a fallen state !
Behold her giant aqueducts and tombs,
Her sculptured arches and vast catacombs !
As ages since the elders of the state
Awaited calmly their impending fate,
And armed alone with symbols of the law
Inspired the rude barbarians with awe—
Thus Rome herself now stands, unarmed, yet
       grand,
Amidst the relics of her lost command,

Whilst ruin halting, hesitates to ply
The final stroke upon such majesty!"

Thus muses Claudio, as from Alba's shade
He marks the well-known scene, so soon to fade
Amidst the mem'ries that like spirits cling
Around the sepulchres from which they spring;
For through the land at last the whisper runs,
Calling from schemes to action all her sons!

Far as can range the beauty-stricken eye,
Fair hills, in rainbow circlet, bound the sky,
Save where upon the turquoise gleaming west
The heav'ns bend down to kiss the ocean's
    breast.
Cimino's range of branching Apennine,
And far La Tolfa's amethystine line,
Soracte's ridge, round which the severed plain
Sweeps circlingly to meet its own again;
Sabina's crests, Alban's volcanic height—
All, girt around Campagna, guard the site
Of Rome—who, like a captive shackled, stands
Clasped in the glittering Tiber's golden bards.

Time-severed aqueducts from fissures throw
Their wasted streamlets upon tombs below ;
Or, ruin-choked, their futile channels bear,
Reared upon trains of arches through the air,
Converging towards the distant domes and
    walls
On which the splendour of the sunlight falls,
And where the ringed arena seems to wed
The mourning city to her glorious dead !

" Farewell ! belovèd haunts of happy hours !
Farewell ! ye Iris-hued Campagna flow'rs !
As echoing vibrations, soft and low,
As scent of roses faded long ago—
Thus sadly mystical how soon will be
This ungrasped dream I call Reality !
How imperceptibly 'twill pale and die,
To swell the shadowy ranks of Phantasy."

And then he travels on—till struggling light
Of evening yields day's sceptre to the night :
Then on again, as an avenging day
Subdues the darkness with a golden ray.

On—where Cisterna's watchful towers command
The dreary Pontine's pestilential land,
Confronting grimly the insidious foe
That lurks unseen amid the plains below.

Across the marshes—hurriedly again—
Where twenty cities silently have lain
For centuries. Where long grass rustling waves
Above unmarked innumerable graves.
A nation's burial ground! where vapours creep
Like waves upon the agitated deep,
Or, like battalions of uneasy shades,
Whose unsubstantial forms as daylight fades,
Flit noiselessly, and with sepulchral breath
Insnare fresh victims to their fields of death.

Then on where Terracina's dwellings creep
Beneath the shelter of the Volscian steep,
As though commingled with the golden sand,
The sea had washed white pearls upon the
    land!
Where gloomy Itri and grim Fondi lie
In wildly mountainous obscurity;

Then down upon the glowing shore below
Where stood the villa home of Cicero,
And where the lingering orange-trees of old,
Still lace their boughs and toss their balls of
  gold.
Past lone Minturnæ's now deserted walls,
Near which—reluctant—Garigliano falls
Into the bosom of the sea, then on
Where Casilinum is now built upon ;
And thus still onward to where Naples rests,
Beneath Vesuvius' fire-emitting crests
Appearing lovely in her tranquil bliss,
As Venus sleeping in the arms of Dis.

III.

The angel of the night outspreads her wings
Above the City of the Bay.   All things
Are hushed and tranquil.   On the tow'r-crowned
     walls
The opalescence of the moonlight falls,
But 'neath each roof, within each deep recess,
The darkness creeps to hide its nothingness,
And as the way-worn traveller descends
A labyrinthian Vicolo, that wends
Its way to the Toledo, dark and tall
His shadow stalks upon the neighbouring wall
In weird companionship, whilst faltering on
His slow steps blot the light they rest upon,
And to his ear the still air seems imbued
With breathings of the sleeping multitude.

Sudden across his path a red gleam falls
From a recess within th' adjacent walls,
Where 'neath a hoary archway, guarded by
Two cherubim in sculptured imagery,

Some steps, that worshippers by prayers and
    tears
Have consecrated through unnumbered years,
Ascend towards an Altar, bathed in light,
For ever shining on throughout the night,
Where, all resplendent in a jewelled sheen,
Appears an image of the heavenly Queen ;
Her bleeding heart transfixed with swords of
    woe—
The types of anguish suffered long ago ;
Her hands in patient agony comprest
Upon her pierced and lacerated breast ;
Her eyes turned—as in ecstasy—above,
With resignation and adoring love.

Before the shrine, within the rays that shed
A holy nimbus round her bending head,
A maiden, weeping, kneels. Her face is pale,
E'en near the shimmering whiteness of the veil,
That squarely plaited o'er her forehead lies,
And models to her form its draperies.
Beneath its folds, the radiance here and there
Steals loving touches from her raven hair,

And lingering on her peasant garb imbues
The scarlet and the blue with warmer hues.
Claudio in silence gazes, and then low
Before the Altar bends.

       Upon her brow
Tracing the cross, the girl arises calm—
But starts at sight of him in vague alarm,
That lasts not, for her guileless trust is
  given
To one thus bowed in fellowship with Heaven.

Then Claudio rising, meets her gaze with tears
Still dimmed :
    " Fair maid, whate'er thy grief or fears,
Confide them unto me, for by this shrine,
My will already moulds itself to thine."

Sweet accents give response :
         " I trust in thee
For thou art like the saintly forms I see
In frescoed churches.   From a woodland glen
I come, a stranger to these haunts of men,

And fear this wilderness of streets, whence night,
Unfriendly to the maid, has chased the light ;
So here, beneath the bless'd Madonna's eye,
I claim a virgin's right to sanctuary.
But ah ! where Santa Lucia skirts the bay,
I know my sire has watched the livelong day
For my return, and when the Vesper Hymn
Brought not his own loved Silvia back to him,
What anxious thoughts would wound with need-
        less fears
The love that has encompassed all my years ! "

Then thus to her the youth : " Be thou the guide
And I will be protector.   By thy side,
As Ischia over Procida,* o'er thee
I'll watch, nor ever pass the severing sea
Of virtuous respect.   Come, let us hence,
Nor fear to give me all thy confidence."

They leave the shrine together, hand in hand ;
The girl conducts him to the moonlit strand,

---

* Two islands off the shore of Baiæ.

Where music from the coral-gifted sea
Seems echoing some Nereid minstrelsy.
And to that harmony the maiden sets
The idyl of her life, nor ever lets
One discord mar the theme.
                    To him who hears
The even tenor of her life appears
A rosary of pearls—as pure, as fair,—
Of which each day is told away in prayer!

Through wild Calabrian woods the sun has
     smiled
Upon the advent of this peasant child.
A widowed father's tenderness has sealed
Her innocence with filial love—a shield
Immaculate,—whilst in her simple breast
His words, though fraught with superstition, rest
In seeming purity, as light which falls
Through coloured glass upon cathedral walls,
Appears as glorious to th' untutored eye
As when in its untinted unity.
And now upon a pilgrimage they come—
At Naples resting, on their way to Rome.

" Ere yet the Holy City bows again
In mem'ry of the day that Christ was slain—
Within its blessèd walls I lowly trust
That I on bended knees, may press the dust
Of martyrs—that my heart may worship God
Upon the very ground apostles trod,
And all its sins and weaknesses confess
Within th' abode of perfect holiness,—
That Rome may be revealed unto mine eyes
No more in dreams but in realities ! "

Then thus in mournful cadences the youth :
" A dream is ofttimes lovelier than truth ;
It may be wiser not to track the course
Of our delusions to their actual source.
It has been said those beams that warm our
        earth
Are cold within the orb that gives them birth ;
Then maiden be content fulfilled to see
Within thy heart thy dreams of purity."

As when through zephyr-severed boughs a gleam
Of sun lights up the shadows of a stream,

The river trembles at the very breeze
That for the ray breaks passage through the
    trees,—
Thus for an instant in the maiden's breast
The truth illumes, whilst from their wonted
    rest
The waves of doubt are troubled.
                          But the air
Now loses silence and the night-winds bear
A voice of sorrow echoing from afar—
The burden of whose plaint is " Silvia."
The maid replies with an impassioned cry,
" My father! oh! my father! Here am I."
And as a form approaching shades the strand,
She springs to meet and kiss a parent's
    hand :
E'en as a bud which near a rose has lain,
If bent aside springs to the flow'r again !

But scarcely has the gladdened father pressed
The blossom thus recovered to his breast ;
When half mistrustful of his joy a dart
Of winged suspicion pierces to his heart.

"But who is this who with his hand in thine
Thus leads thee through the night?
                              A child of mine
Art thou no longer! From my arms! away!
Are not my years enough, that thou must weigh
Me yet more quickly to the grave with shame?
And thou, base youth, from whate'er source thy
        name,—
However noble or however great,—
A curse henceforth shall mingle with thy fate,
And from a peasant's arm a blow disgrace
In thee, through thee, the fortunes of thy race!"

Then from his quivering hand a stroke descends,
From which the youth shrinks not but rather
        lends
Himself unto, as overcome with woe
The agèd head sinks with the falling blow.

"Old man, allay thy passion and thy fears!
Thine only daughter still shall prop thy years
In innocence! Not thus within my arms
Could I support thee, were thy vague alarms

Founded on aught but love to her!   Arise
And read her purity within her eyes!"

And then—beseeching, with clasped hands,—
    the maid :
" Annul thy curse!   Unsay what thou hast
    said !
Father !   He is my friend, and thine through
    me !
Annul thy curse—lest it should turn to thee
As some malignant spirit seeking rest,
And finding none, returns unto the breast
That sent it forth !"

                    Then leaning on the arm
But late accursed, with slow returning calm
Her father speaks :
                    " May good o'ercome the ill
Invoked upon thee, and may blessings fill
The life I would have sown with curses !   May
The Lord concede me an atoning day
To consecrate to thee !"

                    " That day now dawns,
The youth replies : " Look up, see where the
    Morn's
Pale hands uplift the gloom—that nascent light
Will find me such a wanderer as the night
Now leaves, unless some friendly hand will
    guide
Towards a refuge."

                " Where the plaintive tide
Breaks on the shore of Santa Lucia, stands
A fisher's hut, whose humble roof commands
No comfort, but a shelter.   There we stay,
To rest our weariness upon our way
Of pilgrimage unto the shrines of Rome ;
He who receives us in his lowly home
Will take thee also."
                    Thus the agèd sire ;
Whilst fainter and yet fainter gleams the fire
From red Vesuvius on the whitening bay,
And one by one the stars are called away.

IV.

How soon upon a stream is cast the rose
That ever onward with the current flows,
Until it reach the sea ! And thus—ah ! well !
How soon upon a life may fall the spell
That haunts it evermore ! And as at times
Re-echoing from afar come distant chimes,
Now seeming to be lost, now heard again,
As breezes trifle with their sweet refrain,
Thus does a charm once whispered linger on,
Renewed as often as 't is fancied gone !

Three morns, three noons, three eventides are
    all ;
And yet sufficient for the spell to fall !

Three morns—when midst the tendrils of a vine
Which shrouds her casement, Silvia's arms
    entwine
Dividing them, as like a timid bird
She gazes through the leaves unseen, unheard,

D

Upon a form below, and knows not why
Her heart thus longs to steal a memory
To bless the day.

        Three noons—when o'er the bay
The pilgrim maiden floats bright dreams away
To lose them in the distance! Then—*three
eves—*
When silently a small felucca leaves
The strand, and youth and maiden, side by
    side,
Across the trembling bow of waters glide
To watch the wary fisher's torch-light glow
In luring flashes on the waves below,
Like love's first glances wakening from their
    rest
The dazzled visions of a maiden's breast.

And thus the spell was wrought in three short
    days !
So little time life's brightest season stays !
E'en with the happiest it must fade too soon ;
The longest day has but an instant's noon !

       ×   *   *   *

And now the rest is past ; another sun
Will see the pilgrimage again begun,
And Claudio on the sea.
                              Alone, the maid
At night keeps vigil with her tears, afraid
Of all the years that in a weird array
Look from the future !   Their once glad display
Of hope is gone, and gathering clouds unfold
From what in dawning seemed a mist of gold.

Before her casement the vine's budding leaves
Have lent their shadows to the moon, which
        weaves
Amidst the brilliance of its midnight glow
A phantom garland for the maiden's brow.
The stillness rests so lightly on the bay,
The slightest sound can startle it away,
And touch the heart day's tumult could not move,
As through a waste life rings one note of love.
And thus when suddenly a murmuring flow
Of voices twain is heard—now loud—now low,
(As when the breezes through a forest stir
A whisper from the beech to which the fir

Sonorously responds,) the maiden hears,
And half unconsciously arrests her tears.
She knows the voices well ;—the deeper tone
Is of her sire—Claudio's the softer one.

" My friend, I thank thee for the noble vow
Of service tendered, and which even now
May be fulfilled.   But numerous perils lurk
In the completion of the simple work
That mine will seem.

                    The grace that I demand
Is that thou place these papers in the hand
Of him whose name they bear.   But friend—
        take heed !
Light   as   they   are,   these   papers bear   the
        seed
Of mighty changes, and within them lies
A spark to fire Italian destinies !
And to thyself, if found on thee, they will
Entail a curse ; but I have sworn my will
A sacrifice to Italy, and now
My country claims fulfilment of my vow,
As I of thine."

The deeper tones reply ;
" Fear not ; thy papers, with the memory
Of thy protection to my child, shall rest
Securely guarded at her father's breast."

The listener hears no more, the voices fade
Away into the night, and leave the maid
Once more in silence midst the moonlight glow,
The wreath of shades still traced upon her brow.

V.

An endless avenue ! The Volscian plain
Arrays its poplar hosts in serried train
From Anxur* to Velletri. Not a sound
Breaks through their long battalions ! All
    around
Is hushed, save when at intervals a breeze
Transmits its password through the lines of
    trees !
The trees !—for ever arching on before
In dim perspective,—then advancing more,
(Thus seems it to the wayfarers who press
The road, bewildered by its changelessness,)
Till they divide their seeming arch and sway
Themselves upright,—then dwindle far away
Again to nothingness.
              Across the plain
A long canal conveys its watery train

---

* The ancient name for Terracina.

Beside the avenue, whilst all around
Is chilly marshland, whence no sight or sound
Gives pledge of life.
                    Upon the curveless way
The pilgrims tread, through each alternate ray
Of sun and stroke of shade beneath the trees.

The maiden sighs : " The end for ever flees
Before us, father !   Shall we never gain
The boundaries of this perpetual plain ? "

" God knows its limits, child, and He will be
Our guide until we reach them ; but to me
The end seems not so far—perchance that I
May be the first to reach the boundary ! "

" My father ! would'st thou leave me here
     alone ? "

He looks on her with love : " My little one,
I spoke of life—th' inevitable way
Through which we travel onward day by day
Unto an unknown goal ! "

                    Then sudden light
Illumes the pilgrim's face, as though his
    sight
Received some mirage of the realms that lie
Far off beyond the unknown boundary !
And Silvia trembles, for a flush has ris'n
Upon his brow, as though in search of Heav'n
Life's sanguine current rose.

                    " My father, rest :
I see that thou art weary, for thy breast
Is labouring with thy breath."

                    " We soon shall gain
A resting place," he answers, " for the plain
Holds one small shelter on its outstretched
    palm
At Appii Forum, where the holy balm
Of friendship cheered St. Paul. A saintly band
Will meet me also there, and to the land
Which is eternal bear my soul."
                    The hush
Of silence stays his words, the fever-flush

More deeply brands his brow, whilst every
    vein,
Inflamed with poison from the marshy plain,
Swells lividly beneath the rebel strife
Already waging in the lines of life.

And yet he lingers not, but with the force
Of growing fever still maintains his course
Unfalteringly, whilst faint with weariness
The tearful maiden's trembling footsteps press
The road behind.

    *   *   *   *

            At night the saintly band,
He knew would bear him to the spirit land,
Come for the father, and the maid alone
At Appii Forum sighs, " Thy will be done,"—
And weeps.   Not only *he*, but all the world
Seems dead to her ; and as pale vapours,
    curled
By night winds, stalk the plain, she seems to lie
Upon the threshold of eternity
Amidst expectant shades.

                    And when the day—
The first without him—glides at last away
Relentlessly, affixing time's first seal
Unto the finished life, the thoughts which
      steal
Within her breast seem spectres too! Her
      mind
Sways vaguely with emotions undefined,
That dim the sense of loss; and thus is thrown
A veil by nature over grief—a stone
Upon the sepulchre of woe—to hide
From her—her dead.
                    Then whispering to her side
Come words from kindly wayfarers who stay
Likewise at Appii Forum on their way
Of pilgrimage to Rome.   They—to retrace
Her steps advise the maid, but
                          " By the grace
Of Him," she answers, "Who the fatherless
Protects, I unmolested shall progress
Unto my vow's fulfilment."   And unseen
Upon her heart she folds what late had
      been

The Prince's charge unto her sire, the scroll
Of danger-haunted papers, now the sole
Connecting link between the loved and dead
And her unfriended life, nor ever fled
A carrier dove more purely sheltering
Its secret trust beneath a fluttering wing.

VI.

The dirge is sung—the symbol* light has died,
And Rome proclaims the Saviour crucified.
Then darkness falls upon the earth, and gloom
Upon the hearts of men, and many a tomb
Of saintly thoughts that long have slumberèd
Gives up to life its half-forgotten dead
To kindle holy deeds, and acts abound
Of faith and penitence.

　　　　　　　　Upon the ground
Rome consecrates unto her pilgrims, stand
Their Church and Refuge,† whose plain walls command

---

* During the service preceding the "Miserere" in the Sixtine Chapel, certain lights (grouped into a triangle) are extinguished one by one, excepting the last, which is placed behind the Altar during the singing of the dirge; its removal being emblematical of that dread moment when the Light of the World was quenched.

† Adjoining the Church of La Trinità dei Pellegrini is an hospital, where not only are convalescents received, but in which the pilgrims who visit Rome for the Holy Week are lodged and provided for during a time proportioned to the length of their pilgrimages. On Wednesday, Thursday, and

But little notice, yet full many a tear
More dear to heav'n has ofttimes fallen here
Than in the Vatican.   And thither come
The noblest of the youths and maids of Rome
To work out penitence ; here Maries bend
To wash the travellers' feet ; here Marthas lend
Their kindliness to cheer the pilgrims' fare,
And every word and action seems a prayer.
White 'neath the lamplight gleam the tables,
    spread
With frugal fare of lettuces and bread,
Round which flit graceful figures ministering,
Like fluttering humming-birds upon the wing,
All plumed in black and red.*
                  Th' adjoining hall,
With long-rowed benches flanks its whitewashed
    wall,

Friday in the Holy Week the nobles of Rome perform penance
by washing the wanderers' feet, and ministering to them at the
supper with which the pilgrims are provided after their ablu-
tions.   These two ceremonies are respectively termed the
Lavanda and Cœna.

  * The fair penitents of Rome who take part in this ceremony
are all similarly attired in a most picturesque costume, in which
the pleasing contrast of black and red is conspicuous.

With pilgrims lined, at whose toil-hardened feet
Kneel daughters of patrician Rome, to mete
Their balance against sin.
                                Amidst the troop
Of pilgrims is a maid, of all the group
Most young and fair, with eyes that seem to see
Religion everywhere; but pale is she
And mournful, as Egeria ere her change.
Bowed at her feet soft-touching hands arrange
Her wayworn sandals, and a haughty brow,
—Imperious e'en in servitude—bends low
Before the woodland girl.
                                That brow is set
With hair as golden as a coronet,
And purple eyes that seem made dark with pain,
Through which at times gleams forth a proud
        disdain,
Like light from amethysts. A summer gale
Ne'er bowed before a lily of the vale
A lovelier lily queen !

                        "What fancy, child,
Has lured thy footsteps here? Was not thy wild

Retreat amidst the unpolluted hills
Meet home for thee ?   The psalmody that trills
Within the wood-lark's throat, was it too free,—
Its simple notes too innocent for thee ?
Or was the incense which the guileless flow'rs—
High priests of nature—from their leafy bow'rs
Waft heav'nwards, all too pure, that thou
  should'st come
Unto the rotten pageantry of Rome ?
Oh ! child of faith, beware !   The outward show
Conceals a world of mystery below !
The stately pall with pomp embroidered holds
A corpse enshrouded in its velvet folds !
Approach it not—turn homeward to thy vines,
And when afar the sun reflected shines,
Making St. Peter's dome a sun to thee,
Weep thou, and pray upon thy bended knee
For those beneath its shade."
      The pilgrim maid
Hears with pale wonder on her brow, dismayed,
As they who listen on Campanian ground
With nature's fairest scenery around
To thunders far beneath.

                    Then in reply,
She murmurs timidly;
                     " Thine acts belie
Thy warnings, lady, or thou dar'st not kneel,
As now, in rites thy Church has blessed, nor
    seal
Thy doubts with mockery."
                     " Nay, simple child,"
Such is the curse of Rome.   The soul defiled
By doubt yet wears a mask of faith, and sees
All holy that th' unerring Church decrees!
Insnared by toils of sacerdotal art,
We lose the purest instincts of the heart,
As birds once taught some artificial strain,
In vain recall their own true notes again!
Thou, fresh from nature, may perchance still see
Her truth reflected upon all, but we
See darkness everywhere!   Ah! could'st thou
    know
The bitterness and pride that lurk below
These forms of love!"
                 Then—as the pilgrim hears,
Her wonder changes pityingly to tears;

In faith secure, as on a sea-girt steep
A flower which blooms on rocks that chafe the
    deep,
And which in fragile beauty bending low,
Seems to rebuke the waves which rage below.

As thus she bends, some papers gleaming white
Flit from her peasant-kerchief, and alight
Fluttering upon the ground. With eager hand
Outstretched, the lady grasps their folds, as
    scanned
In one brief glance their superscription sends
A thrill unto her heart.
                        The pilgrim rends
The air with one long cry, as they who see
Hope swiftly struck from life !
                        " Oh ! give them me !
Oh ! give my papers back, for they are all
That now I live for !"   But her accents fall
Upon unpitying ears.
                        " Secure the maid !
The false—the traitorous pilgrim, who has made
Our faith a cloak for treachery, and come

E

Accomplice of the band late fled from Rome,
On rebel mission in a pilgrim guise!
Flame in her heart, religion in her eyes!
On rebel mission! For too well I know
How writes my traitor cousin, Claudio!
A rebel mission! Born, perchance, of love!
Feigned as *I* know he well *can* feign, to move
Her to his aid! Nay, speak not, girl, 'tis vain—
These papers that upon thy breast have lain
Tell far too much!"

                Thus cries the ireful maid,
Unconscious that she also is betrayed
To those who hear, for storms oft bring to shore
Some shell which ocean would for evermore
Have treasured in its depths.

                Then all around;
"The Princess loves him!" breaks in whispered
    sound,
And Silvia, borne half-swooning from the hall,
Hears the low-murmured accents as they fall :
Mournful are they as some chance wind-drawn
    strain
From strings the harpist ne'er shall touch again!

VII.

Spinola's* groves are tipped with shimmering
    light,
And Dian drops the treasures of the night
Between their boughs, till all the ground beneath
Seems flecked with silver seeds.

                Full many a wreath
Of branching olive and festooning vine,
In shadow waves upon the pale moonshine,
In silent concert with the leaves that move
To rustling music in the air above ;
And cypresses, impelled by night winds, bow
Their lofty heads within the melting glow,
As though acknowledging the mute caress
Night lends unto Spinola's loveliness.
Where in a rose-girt space a fountain gleams—
Like some white spirit chained to earth that seems

* The Sicilian expedition under Guiseppe Garibaldi em-
barked on the night of May 5th, 1860, from the Villa Spinola,
near Genoa.

For ever struggling upward to the sky,
Yet ever falling backward murmuringly—
There—silent figures glide across the sward,
In furtive speed, with many a glance toward
The all-surrounding trees, as though there
    were
Some evil lurking in the shadowy air.
Dark forms are they and dim, but they shall
    sway
A nation's destiny, and chase away
A cloud from liberty.
                            Onward they pass,
With steps so stealthy that the treach'rous
    grass
Scarce whispers forth the secret of their tread ;
On, to the strand, where faithless waters spread
Again in welcome at a hero's feet,
As when they rolled Tyrrhènum* waves to meet
The Chief of Troy.

------

* Upon the western coast of Italy the Mediterranean waters
were anciently divided into the Sinus Ligusticus—the Tyrrhènum Mare and the Inferum Mare.

            " My friends, Sicilians wait ! "
It is enough—the Leader's words elate
The men with zeal renew'd, and from the shore
A muster-roll is called, which echoing o'er
Th' assembled groups, unto each name receives
An answering voice. Then as the ocean heaves
In seeming unison with each brave heart,
One after one enfranchised boats depart,
Like sea-birds eager for the storm,—their freight
A people's liberty—a nation's fate !

Prince Claudio, numbered with th' Adventurers,
    sees
His hopes expand—as from the land, the seas,—
Hopes that grow brighter when th' encom-
    passed main
Upon the south is narrowed back again
By Sicily's fair coasts. Now dreams may die
And into deeds of valour fructify !
The time has come to summon forth the dead,
T' unbind each fettered hand, each shrouded head,
That from the sepulchre wherein they lie
May rise the stricken hearts of Italy.

Marsala first to the Deliverer droops
The tyrant flag, and the avenging troops
March unresisted through the town.

                             At dawn
Toward Salemi's walls the men are drawn,
Expectant of the forces said to lie
Near to Calatafimi threat'ningly ;
And *there* at length they meet.

                        Now clouds of sand,
Aroused by conflict, eddy round the hand
That wages death, and hovering o'er the fray—
Like some expectant vulture o'er its prey—
Dust circles round what soon to dust shall turn.
As when sun-parched the western prairies burn,
Compelled at last to flame and shoot on high
Avenging fires to the malignant sky—
Thus blaze this day in Sicily the hearts
That wrong has kindled, till the oppressors'
    darts
Before the wrath aroused shrink back and yield
The vict'ry of Calatafimi's field.
Then, where should pour the Amiraglio's flood
Upon the dried-up stones, fall drops of blood,

To witness silently of wrong and pain,
Till Heaven's pure tears shall wash away the
 stain.
And as of old the seven times circled walls
Fell at the trumpet blasts of faith, so falls
Palermo's* pride before the sevenfold cry,
Wrenched from a desperate people's agony.
Soon—bowed before th' avowed resistless fate—
Milazzo offers to capitulate,
And from Messina's port glide one by one
The hostile ships of war.
 Then all is done ;
And Freedom guided by the hand of God,
Treads jubilant upon Sicilian sod.

---

* " According to the admission of Neapolitan officers of rank,
their forces at Palermo consisted of no less than 24,000 men."—
Extract from " The Garibaldians in Sicily," by Alexander Dumas.
Garibaldi's band at this time numbered not more than 1,400 men.

VIII.

Where   chestnut   woods,   beyond   Palermo's
    walls,
Climb grassy knolls, and trickling water-falls
In freedom revelling, babble loud and leap
Foaming in wanton glee from steep to steep,
Like silver ladders up the mountain heights ;
Where all the colours of the southern lights
Are spread, from their prismatic band untied,
Seeming in rich confusion multiplied ;
There—built in mockery of light and space—
A Prison mars the charm of Nature's face ;
Showing where misery and sin have trod—
Man's shadow on the glorious work of God !

Those   crested   tow'rs, pregnant   with   human
    woe,
Rose on yon sunny slope long years ago,
But never until now has Freedom's breath
Forestalled the gloomy liberator Death !

The gates are burst! The free air rushes in!
Mark the wan groups that once again begin
Upon the threshold of their tomb to live!
Who pausing shrink, and wonderingly give
A resurrection gaze! Whilst they who stand
Without, stretch forth to them a helping hand,
And proffer guidance to the steps that reel
With unaccustomed liberty.
                                        Then kneel
The Rescued, joined by their Deliv'rers, bowed
In an adoring, a rejoicing crowd.

But some there are so broken down with
        pain
They scarcely care to quit those walls again,
Their lives imbittered by some tyrant care
That leaves no freedom for them anywhere.
Friends have they lost perchance, or hope, or
        youth,
Or some illusion which they held as truth.
"Then why," think they, "should we forsake
        the cell
That all our vigils and our tears could tell,

And which seems — echoing ceaselessly our
    cries !—
More faithful than are human sympathies ?"

These hopeless ones the Liberators seek
Within the too familiar walls, and speak
To them reviving words, to stimulate
The stagnant life-blood, and if not too late
Restore the harmonies which wrong has riven
That should attune their hearts to hope and
    heaven !

With them, piercing anew the Dungeon's gloom,
Claudio tracks forth the steps—his heart the
    doom—
Of captives who have languished year by year
Within that rank and mildewed atmosphere—
For e'en the purity of heaven's free air
Is blighted when it only passes there !
To him each oozy drop of damp that falls
Upon his forehead from the vaulted walls
Appears the spirit of a tear of woe
Wrung from some prisoner's eyelid long ago ;

Each red-hued lichen seems a mark of blood,
Still lingering where once swept a human
    flood,
And on the walls where clammy damp-stains lie,
Appears engrained a sweat of agony.
E'en daylight pales in terror of the place,
Where doors unbarred yield some unwonted
    space
Through which to slip a gleam, and trembling
    lies
Across the prison's dank intricacies.

One such faint glimmer Claudio traces where
The walls divide on an ascending stair,
So steep, so narrow, that it seems to lie
Within the thickness of the masonry.
Above, its bolt withdrawn, an open door
Reveals a cell beyond, with rush-strewn floor,
On which the sunbeams through a loop-hole
    glow—
Gilding the passage Man has wrought for Woe!
Stretched on the rushes where the ray can trace
The tender beauty of her upturned face,

A maid unconscious lies—a fever brand
Upon her brow, as though a heavenly hand,
Impatient for another angel, twined
Celestial roses there.   All unconfined,
Her tresses in an ebon tracery rest
Inlaid upon the ivory of her breast,
As if the meshes of that silken net
Were loth to free the gentle spirit yet.

" Silvia !   My guileless Silvia here ?   Alas !
Could not the rancour of our tyrants pass
Such innocence as thine ?   Awake !   Arise !
See how at last upon our destinies
The Heav'ns look kind !   Their will was ever
      thine—
Then smile with them upon us—Silvia mine !"

If it be true that every word must chase
Perpetual echoes through eternal space—
That sounds which seem to us to fade and die
Are rushing onwards everlastingly—
Perchance the many utterances of love
Unheard on earth, may yet in realms above,

Launched to infinity—in ceaseless roll—
Flash with swift comfort past their destined
    soul !
But now unheeded is the pleading cry
Of love and anguish, and the echoes fly,
Striking confused against the prison walls
Till they escape to Heav'n, whilst Claudio
    falls
Bowed at the maiden's side with wild appeals
Of yearning tenderness.

                    Then, as he kneels,
His gaze upon her face, the air is stirred
Softly around her lips by one faint word—
She knows him not, and yet her spirit clings
Unto *his* name amidst its wanderings !

Footsteps without approach, the stair ascend,
And Claudio's comrades group around their
    friend.
Raising the maiden with most tender care
They—forming into sad procession—bear
Her to the world without, where dewy grass
Hushes the martial footsteps as they pass,

And where the red shirts struck by sunlight
    stand
Girt round their burden like a fiery band.
A vesper bell from some adjacent height
Floats music to the plain—a lingering light
Glints on the chestnut woods from tree to tree—
Like glancing spray upon a wind-tossed sea—
And lines of purple and of golden red
Trace mystic writing on the sky o'erhead,
As though the sunset with inscribing ray
Noted the records of the finished day.

IX.

Advancing from the coast a headland stands
Alone before the sea, with gorgeous bands
Of verdure circling its majestic crown
And red-hued precipices sloping down
Sheer to the azure deep.   It seems to be
Some great high-priest of that untroubled sea,
Standing barefooted by the veil that lies
In envious folds above its mysteries.
Half up the mountain side a white arcade
Springs from the sandstone cliff, with hollowed
        shade
Beneath each arch and with uneven piers,
Now caught upon a spur of rock that rears
A jagged outline, fringed with prickly pear,
Now lengthening into long white columns, where
They dip to some abyss.
                        A convent wall
Above the arches, unadorned and tall,
With narrow windows dotted here and there—
Bewildering motes upon a dazzling glare !—

Bared to the ardour of the southern light,
Stands stern, as some world-wearied anchorite,
Confronting heav'n alone.

               A mighty screen
Behind arises in an emerald sheen
Of ilex and of cypress branches spread
Upon the slanting summits overhead—
A barrier that the gentle nuns have set
Between them and the world they would forget.

In this retreat, beneath the Sisters' care,
Young Silvia trembles back to life—a prayer
Upon her lips, as though a breath of heaven
Escaped the gates death has so nearly riven.
Feebly at first her opening eyelids fix
Upon a figure of the crucifix
Suspended near, then from the form divine
Turn slowly to the watchful Ursuline
Bent o'er her couch;

              "Are still my fancies vain,
Or have they wandered back to truth again?
These are no prison walls,—nor this the air
That sapped my life with hourly poison there!

Tell me—is this of earth—this odorous breath
That fresh from summer roses entereth
Fanning my brow, as though an angel wing
To me invisible were ministering?"

"Forget thy prison, child, and calm thy dread;
Both real woes and fevered dreams have fled.
The Blessèd Virgin, watchful of thy fate,
Had thee conveyed unto the convent gate
Of sainted Ursula ; and constantly
We sisters tend on thee, alternately,
Fasting—that thou may'st live ; whilst day and
    night,
Within our chapel burns a constant light,
Placed by thy friend upon the altar there,
The ardent symbol of his ceaseless prayer."

"Alas ! I have no friend ! The steadfast flame
Would scarcely burn if placed in Silvia's name !
A peasant girl am I—loved but by *one*,
And he has left me in the world alone !
My father gone—defenceless and obscure—
I learnt how even Rome may wrong the pure—

F

Condemned, untried, for evermore to lie
Within the prison vaults of Sicily !"

" Poor child !   But still believe me there is yet
A friend left unto thee ; can'st thou forget ?
To us poor sisters memory seems to press
So vividly upon our weariness !
There is no outer world for us, to win
Our thoughts from dwelling on the world
     within.
A fond face seen in the far days of yore
Wears the same smile to us for evermore ;
And loving words, though whispered years ago,
Ne'er lose the accents that entranced us so.
Ah ! child ! sometimes methinks that it is well
To be a nun within a convent cell !"

Then Silvia falteringly :
                    " There once was one
Who found me—lost in Naples—all alone ;—
I knew him but three days—'twould be too
     vain
To dream that we should ever meet again."

And yet—can it be Hope ?—The life-blood
    streams,
Renewed and kindled through her veins ;—it
    seems
As though vibrations from a chord of sound
Had sent fresh harmonies to echo round,
And charm all thoughts of pain, as grains of
    sand   .
Shake into form beneath an unseen hand
At stroke of melody.
                    Silent she lies,
Dropping the veiling lashes on her eyes
To shut in all her joy ; whilst lingering there,
The nun, still watchful, steals in rapid prayer
A Pater Noster from her beads, and signs
The symbol of the cross in mystic lines.

X.

The gorgeous southern autumn lies oppressed
Amidst its own delights. The vague unrest
Of calm hangs subtly in the golden air,
And all the distances and hill-tops wear
A veil—that seems of neither mist nor haze—
But wearied colour shrinking from the blaze
And seeking rest afar.

                The purple vines
On terraces of rock, in serried lines,
Await their sacrifice, and bending low
The citron branches to the ground below
Let fall their topaz fruit. The path which
    leads
Unto the convent gate is strewed with seeds—
The summer burden of the wearied trees,—
And ever and anon a lizard flees
Across its stony windings, mute and fleet,—
An elfish spirit of the silent heat !

But o'er the rough-hewn pavement, stretched before
The whitened archway of the convent door,
A cypress marks its shade in ebon line,
Tracing a limit to the bright sunshine.

A time-worn parapet of stone defends
The mountain platform, where the cliff descends
Abruptly to the sea, and resting there,
With brow uncovered to the breathless air,
Claudio awaits.
        Thus through the summer gone,
Full oft the youth has lingered there alone,
To watch St. Ursula's closed walls, wherein
His love—she whom the angels strove to win—
So nearly strayed to heav'n ; and later, when
She turned unto her own sweet life again,
He oft has met beneath the cypress shade,
Led by the kindly nuns, his peasant maid ;
And sometimes—as to one from whom they hold
Their charge,—they her to him have brought and told,

With garrulous simplicity and tears,
Of all her sufferings and of all their fears,
Whilst she all pale and silent trembled near,
Too vaguely happy, too confused to hear
Their speech, yet conscious that at each farewell
His eyes would meet her timid ones, and tell
That silent story which can still entrance
Long after words have lost significance.

But now this autumn noon, with full intent
To give to looks a voice, the youth has sent
Unto the Abbess, and a sanction won
To see alone his Silvia ere the sun
Shall close the ardour of his golden eye
Upon the coasts of sea-girt Sicily.

The cypress shade more to the eastward creeps,
Leaving a pathway that the sunlight steeps
In gold for her who comes. Throughout the air
A trembling stirs, as though its pulses were
Awakened by the gentle form that now
Stands doubtfully, as though uncertain how
To pass the virgin gate.

With reverence given
When love in love can see a light from heaven,
The youth approaches where the maiden stands
And lifts unto his lips the tight-clasped hands
That closely twined upon her bosom, press
Back to her heart its flood of happiness.

" When, Silvia, borne from Santa Lucia's shore
I left thee (thinking we should meet no more !)
Unmindful that so near the Sirens'* caves
Enchantment still might float upon the waves,
Thy charms I vainly trusted to forget—
But ah ! their spell is lingering round me yet !
How often absence weaves a lasting tie
From what seems scarce enough for memory !
Methinks that thoughts are wanderings of the
    soul,
Which, when at times evading the control
Of mortal ties, meets those for whom it yearns !
Re-unions that the earth-bound frame discerns

---

* The Sirens are said to have inhabited the rocky coasts of
the islands of Sirenusæ.

But dimly when our life with labour teems—
In sleep, seen vividly, we call them dreams.
Thus we have met, my Silvia, and I greet
Thee now, not only as a maiden sweet
Seen three short days, but as one loved and
    known,
Whose soul has held communion with mine own.
I ask not if it seemeth thus to thee,
For wherefore tremblest thou in meeting me ?
What truth but one, could bend that candid brow,
Which never surely learnt to droop till now ?
Ah ! raise thine eyelids, sweet, for they reveal
All by thus low'ring that they would conceal."

As laden flowers from dewy languor rise
Beneath the blessing of the morning skies,
Her soft eyes tremble upwards unto his
To lose their love-drops in a tender kiss.

     *   *   *   *

Half from her lips — half from the love that
    learns,
As if by intuition, and discerns

What is by love withholden, Claudio gains
The maiden's history of the fatal plains—
The journey on to Rome—the meeting there
With the Princess, to whom his papers were
Her mute betrayers. Then to her he gives
The future he has planned,—a dream that lives
Alas ! but in his breast. For him, one year
Of glorious war,—whilst she, free from all fear,
Shall tarry with the nuns—then, Naples free,—
Rome, Queen of a united Italy,—
And Silvia his bride !

               " Till then our love
Must trust ; and, sweetest, when the sun above
Looks down on thee, think how its light has
     sped
Through trackless space to shine upon thy
     head !
Think how the stars through myriads of miles
Have sent the rays that watch upon thy smiles !
Mark how the ocean waters haste to meet,
And kiss, when thou art near, thy wandering
     feet :

Thus may'st thou easily believe that I
Shall worship with no less idolatry!"

And thus together where the cliff is set
With bordering of ruined parapet,
The lovers linger, whilst the golden day
Hurries the sweetness of their lives away.

XI.

In all excess of gladness or despair
The soul within us is compelled to prayer;
For like those subtle influences which move
The ocean deep and raise the flood above,
There is at times a holy impulse given
That draws the waters of the soul to Heaven!

Alone with all her joy—the one distress
Of parting lost in love and happiness,—
The maid, bewildered with a sense of light,
(As one half dazzled by a meteor's flight,
Who recks not that the flash of splendour flown
Leaves nought behind it but a cold grey stone,)
Seeks in the convent chapel sanctuary
For all her new-born bliss.
                                        The shadows lie
Around her in a silence still and deep,
For vesper hymns have hushed the day to
    sleep,

But lights upon the holy Altar shine,—
Now caught by silver bars around a shrine,
Now striking arch, or shaft of porphyry,
Or polished forms of sculptured imagery,
Until with special brilliancy they fix
In halo round a jewelled crucifix.

And silent kneels the maid—no utterance robs
Her lips of motion, yet her being throbs
In rapt communion.
                         Burn the lights more pale?
Before the glittering crucifix a veil
Seems for an instant drawn! But now again
'Tis gone, as catching up the golden rain
The cross shines forth once more.
                         Yet something creeps—
A shadow midst the shades—a form that steeps
Itself in dimness! Near where Silvia kneels
It glides, screening the altar blaze, as steals
A cloud upon the moon! The blessèd trance
Breaks off its ecstasy in fear! One glance
And terror fixes in her eyes! for there
Before her, still majestic, but less fair,

Stands the Princess of Rome!
    " Speak not—nor fear:—
I come to save thee, child—*to save !* Do'st
 hear ?
To save thee from thy folly and thy crime ;
To crush thy joy indeed, as thou hast mine,
But still to save thee from a greater woe,
As purgatory from the hell below.
The first thou art not that a coronet
Has dazzled from her sphere. Renounce !
 Forget !"

Then Silvia rises, all her terror gone,
And indignation in her eyes alone !
" What is my folly, lady ? what my sin ?
Is it that *I*, a peasant girl, dare win
The love thy lineage could not gain for thee ?
The greatness of thy noble world would be
Indeed most potent could it buy the heart,
And win with gold the soul !
      My foe thou art
In that he loves me, but believe me I
Have won my happiness unwittingly !

And by this shrine I vow, if it could be,
I'd give the heart that I have gained to thee
For his dear sake, for it were better far
That he should wed with thee than Silvia."

"*If it could be!*   How art thou so secure?
Believest thou men love for evermore?"

" E'en if they do not, what is past is true;
The future changes, but cannot undo.
A love one instant ours unchanged will be
Ours for that instant through eternity!
What boots it in the never-ceasing roll
Of countless ages, if the yearning soul
Looks to a past of earthly hours or years?
By depth, not length, 't will mete its joys and
    tears!"

" If thus it be, child, thou do'st then possess
Secure what thou hast gained of happiness.
But ask no more, and for his sake untwine
The threads from his life that have tangled
    thine.

Take thy short dream to bless thy future
    years,
And risk not to outweigh its sweets with tears.
Think not that when upon thy lowly brow
His jewels shine, he'll love thee then as now,
Ah ! no ! thy sylvan loveliness will set
Beneath the splendours of a coronet,
And he will blush and thou wilt weep to see
How rude the charms he once so praised in
    thee !' "

" Oh ! lady, spare me ! for my dazzled eyes
Have scarce yet turned away from paradise,
And of the sun they just have looked on bear
Bright images that hover everywhere.
Disturb them not.   Leave me my joy and go.
Hast thou not worked on me sufficient woe ?
'Twas thou betrayed me ! 'twas thy influence
    strove
In those dread vaults to hide me from my
    love !
But e'en the cruel prison proved to be
More kind than thou—it gave him back to me.

And yet—thy bitter words might prove too
    true!
Oh! Holy Virgin! than that he should rue
His choice, far better that to grief and pain
I turn my long accustomed life again!
For not one pang that in the future lies
Could wound as scorn in his once tender
    eyes!"

Is it a smile exultant that appears
To move th' austerity of her who hears?
And yet the sweetness of her voice belies
All that there is of triumph in her eyes!

" Maiden, why speak of sorrow or of pain?
Within these convent walls there long have
    lain
The graves of many a wordless memory
Untouched by all its former agony!
Graves—round which flowers have grown—
    where sunlight gleams
Round which the gentle nuns weave golden
    dreams—

Join thine to theirs—'tis safer here than where
The rude world breathes its desecrating air!"

" Princess, away! Thy persecution cease!
Enough—for thou hast poisoned all my peace!
Go—thou hast conquered, and thy lover free,
The Future take—but leave the Past to me!"

XII.

The moon has risen ;—o'er the watery plain
The radiance striking seems to rend in twain
The ocean veil, and through the fissure show
Glories escaping from the depths below.
Pale on the steep cliff gleams the convent
    wall
—Paling as though in fear—as gathering all
Her shades around her, steady night creeps on.

Alone before her casement—pensive—wan—
The Princess stands — leaning with folded
    arms,
And sighing with the sea.
                  The auburn charms
Of her bright hair are tossed aside ; her face
Is ominous with thoughts of ill that chase
Away its loveliness ; and from her eyes
The evil star which rules her destinies,
Strikes a reflected gleam.

A passion-flower
Bent with its dewy burden, from a bower
Above her casement twined, stoops down to rest
Its languid petals on her heaving breast.
Fiercely upon her heart she crushes them!
" Thus would I crush all passion and contemn
All love! Why should our nature upon earth
Bring so much ill? What influence at the birth
Of man brings with the beauties of his soul
The subtle evil that must mar the whole?
Once—was there ought within my breast but
    peace?
Aught but the tenderest wishes to increase
All happiness, or where I met with pain
Give back the sunshine of the heart again?
I can remember—'tis not long ago—
My being shuddering at a cry of woe!
And yet before that peasant maiden's cry,
Wrung from her terror and her agony,
When to my hands her papers fell—all light,
All sympathy fled from my soul, and night
Absorbed my life! What joy it was to feel
My rival in my power! To set my seal

Upon her anguish ! To a prison cell
Consign her charms !—Call I these joys ? Ah !
    well !
Joys were they not, but rather triumphs, set
Like jewels in a poisoned coronet,
That round the brow with fatal radiance twine,
Racking with deadly torture whilst they shine !
And all my wariness has been in vain !
My schemes but giv'n her back to him again,
And interposed a mightier barrier still
Between his heart and mine ; for though *her* will
Before my stronger one already bows,—
(Nor will I leave this convent till her vows
Chain her for ever here !) yet what of *his ?*
Will her woe bring me nearer to my bliss ?"

And for all answer to the question came
A restless murmur from the deep—the same
Response there ever has been and shall be
To human hearts till there be " no more sea."

XIII.

Meanwhile to Naples Claudio speeds, com-
    pelled
To join again the patriot band, now swelled
In conquests as in force.
                        Redeemed and free,
High from her fort proud Naples waves the
    three
Loved colours with their cross—the flag that
    springs
From dauntless faith and noble sufferings!
The Bourbon rule has perished as the blight
A thunder storm clears off within a night,
Leaving the fruit to ripen in the sun
Of an untainted day.
                    The work is done—
But much to do remains—much to withstand—
Much to consolidate—and much command!
The conquered—desperate and menacing—
The succoured—clamorous for everything!

The Pioneer of liberty needs all
His utmost strength, and prompt to every
    call,
On fields more treacherous now than those of
    war,
Must his supporters stand.
                    Momentous are
The records of the last wild throes that
    bring
Forth Freedom from a nation's suffering.

    *   *   *   *   *   *

There comes a calm at last—dissensions cease;
Each grievance glides into the light of peace.
Then Claudio who through all has held a
    sweet
Anticipation at his heart, to meet
His Silvia prepares.
                    Severed indeed
Have been the lovers, for the heart can read
Less than it dreams, and from the heart the
    source
Of his and the young peasant's intercourse

Alone could spring—whilst that her love could
    rise
To consummation in self-sacrifice,
He knew not nor divined.

               How little trace
Of un-remitting change upon the face
Of self-renewing nature!   Leaves that grew
Last year and fell and witherèd, renew
Themselves and fade upon the self-same tree
To bud—to pale—to fall again and flee
Again 'twixt death and life!
               To Claudio
The time that bloomed and died one year
    ago
Seems risen to charm again, its golden light
Untarnishèd, and all its splendour bright,
As though three hundred and three score of
    suns
Had not died out from time.
               The lizard runs
Swift as of yore across his path and cling
The grapes in purple bunches clustering

Unto the vines renewed ; but as he nears
The convent's guardian cypresses, he hears
Sounds unaccustomed and confused, which
　　greet
His ear where last alone his Silvia's sweet
And loving accents toned their long farewell.
Footsteps re-echoing from the paved court tell
Of crowds unusual there and blend with sound
Of voices—now subdued and rare—now wound
And intermixed upon a chanted chord,
Whilst ever and anon an organ laud
With music shivers the harmonious air,
That groans with melody and in despair
Swoons on the distant hills.

　　　　　　　　　　　Within the gate
The traveller pauses all amazed !　Why wait
These peasants grouped about the chapel door,
And knotted round the court ?　A crowd of poor,
Who scarce would throng so num'rusly to
　　hear
The simple service of the nuns, nor wear
Their gala dress save at some holy feast
Of which none falls to-day.

He stands where least
The pressure of the crowd, and asks,
"What means
All this assemblage gathered here? What scenes
Enact the nuns that to their solitude
And pious rites allure this multitude?"
A beldam leaning near shakes forth reply:—
"We come to see a new-vowed sister lie
Upon her bier, whilst yet in flush of life;
Without the kindly numbness that is rife
In my old limbs—which takes from them the
        sting
Of every pang,—but fresh for suffering
Of mind or sense!"

"A blithe sight truly, dame!
'Twere better fate to be content to claim
The happiness allowed on earth, and not
Grasp at celestial sweets the Heav'ns allot
Only beyond the grave! But who is she
Who thinks to win eternal peace and flee
From sin and woe? As though a convent wall
Could shut out thoughts of ill, or veils could fall

On heart-pursuing memories! Alas!
Both sin and grief are subtle ills that pass
With life alone! pray Heav'n that even then
The soul evade them! But I ask again,
Who is the victim in this sacrifice?"

To him this time a shepherd youth replies:
"Her name we know not, but the country
        teems
With strange reports concerning her; — of
        schemes
In which she shared—of dire imprisonment,—
Of rescue, by the brave deliverers sent
To this poor Sicily—and 'tis all this
Attracts us here. Some say — perchance
        amiss,—
That she is forced to take the veil, and some
Aver that since she came, a dame from Rome
Has followed, to induce her to the vow   .
Through rivalry in love."
                                Tis only now,
As though arousèd by the word of love,
That Claudio wakes unto the truth.

Above,
Unchanged the sun, unchanged the autumn
    sky—
The organ peals still strike forth melody—
The aged crone leans on her staff unmoved—
The shepherd's lips are scarcely yet removed
From the last shape his words have giv'n—
                     and yet
Eternity seems passed, and chaos set
Within the timeless age !
              Now he has driven
Aside with thrusts the wedgèd crowd—has riven
An entrance through the chapel gates, and gained
An access through the throng within—proclaimed
By cries from those whom passion-tossed he flings
Madly aside.
           The chanting chorus sings
Confused to discord—lapsing in a wail—
The priests officiating pause and quail
An instant at the sudden storm, then stand
Confronting with proud gestures of command
Th' intruder—who has gained the altar now
And cries to Silvia to withhold her vow.

Beyond a grating's gilded traceries
Upon the marble ground a coffin lies,
Round which like effigies, that summer suns
Touch not, are ranged in sable band, the nuns;
A low moan answers from their midst—and
    slow,
As though a half-numbed corpse shook off the
    woe
Of death, beneath the pall a figure moves,
And Silvia rising, looks on him she loves.
"Claudio, forget me!   Uncompelled and free
I rob my life of happiness!—of thee!
And if it be a sin to break the vow
I made to thee, an oath more solemn now
Forbids a weightier perjury!—Farewell!
Forget the Silvia thou hast loved too well!
There is another worthier than I
To share with thee thy lofty destiny!
Take *her*—the brilliant Princess!—who will
    give
Thy life a suited fellowship, and live
More nobly blest with thee, than now; whilst I
Can love thee only well enough—to die!"

Then to the funeral couch where she has lain
Her shadowy form sinks slowly down again ;
Whilst wailing rises and a tremor runs
Throughout the rigid company of nuns.
Closely they press around the coffin—weep
And wring their hands—the " maid has fall'n
    asleep "—
Lost unto them as to the world, and wooed
By Death to a celestial sisterhood.

XIV.

Grey gleams the day upon Rotondo's height—
Dim with a weight of tears.

                   The ashen light
Strikes on the host of olive trees that wield
Their limbs distorted, and with silver shield
Give battle to the morn.

                   A vapoury sea
Blots out the plain below, where Rome should be—
Foretokening her doom!—whilst heav'n above
Teems with battalions of fierce clouds which
    move
Like dragons belching steam—with wings out-
    spread,
Or spirits of the City's mighty dead
Stirred at the breath of war!

                A moving shade,
Deepening the greyness of the mount, is laid
Nigh to the olives on Rotondo's slope—
A shadow small—yet big with weighty hope—

It is the patriot camp.

               Confusèd sound
Creeps from it numbly as the moistened ground
Gives back the heavy tread of martial trains,
And hoarse commands,—choked by the rushing
    rains—
Come struggling through the storm; whilst
    bugle cries,
Finding no echo in the laden skies,
Grow faint, and seem to call with muffled breath
Not unto victory, but unto death.

Far off — below — Campagna's cloud-veiled
    grounds
Send up a wind-wave of responding sounds
From a far mightier host — and trembling
    runs
Through the long silent plains, as heavy guns
Drag the arousèd soil; but over all,
Impenetrable hangs the ashen pall
Of mist—a seeming void—from which the hum
Of light-toned clarion and dull beating drum
Comes like an echo from the classic past,

When from another Rome battalions vast
Marched thus on liberty.

                  To meet their foe—
Now from the mount unto the plain below
The patriots descend—unflinching all—
Though to the Papal mercenaries small
And weak in number, as the gleams of light
A sunset leaves to wrestle with the night,
Compared with the star army that the sky
Leads forth upon the day's last agony.

The battle bursts—and loud-voiced havoc thrills
More fierce than storm-gust to the grey-tipped hills
That bow themselves before the clouds and stand,
Like mediators for their blood-stained land,
Veiled, between earth and heav'n.

                  From foe to foe
Flash fiery tokens, scattering as they go
Pain, desolation, death!—Triumphant cries
Unheeded fade to moaning agonies!
Young hearts—unknown of pain—spring forth
    to meet
Prostrating thrusts—and by the eager feet

Of their own comrades—hurrying to the strife,
Have their last pulses trampled from their
  life!
Torn standards fall upon the plain and dye
Their folds with life-blood of the enemy,
Till, as the living fail, each flag is hid
By the staunch dead in faithful pyramid.
And 'tis for only *this* the gates of Rome,
Seen through long years are reached! From
  Peter's dome
At last the free hour promises to sound,—
But 'tis for those who die! The Latin ground
Sucks its deliverers' blood and soon shall
  scent
Its reckless flow'rs with that dear nourishment.
Pressed by o'erwhelming force the patriots
  yield
At last the vict'ry of Mentana's field!
Each backward step out-weighed by deadly
  blows,—
Each bosom turned to the advancing foes,—
No bugler left to sound defeat's last call,—
No trumpeter to herald forth their fall!

H

Retreating to the hills whence they have
    come—
With wistful eyes strained to the end towards
    Rome !

   *   *   *   *   *   *

The day is over, and the setting sun,
As though remorseful for the havoc done,
Is reddening in the west. The morning rain
Has ceased and dried upon the war-stained
    plain ;
And all the mist has rolled far out to sea,
Leaving the wide Campagnian desert free.

Upon an outpost of the mountain steep,
Where blackened olives, seared with battle,
    keep
A silent guard,—stretched on the barren soil—
His head supported by the roots which coil
Like serpents in the sand, a soldier lies,—
His sword still grasped, although his enemies
Have left him there alone—a helpless prey
To one no human weapon keeps away !

A shade of pain has dimmed the youthful glow,
And war-brands sear the once unfurrowed brow,
But yet the subtle notes of nature show
The wounded warrior to be Claudio.

Fixed on the distant west, his eager eyes
Drink in their last of sight where crimsoned
    skies
Throw out the form of Rome.

               Like mystic signs
Engraved upon an Eastern ring, the lines
Irregular of walls and towers arise,
Fraught with a great Past's silent histories,
On the red scroll of heav'n !

              " Is this the end ?
Do all youth's dreams and manhood's struggles
    tend
Only to this ?   Stands Rome thus mute—thus
    calm,
Extending for us no avenging arm ?
Can she thus see her suffering martyrs die—
Thus witness the last pangs of liberty—

And give no sign?   Make not for us one moan?
Of all her palaces stirs not one stone?
Rome—Rome arise!   If all thy Life has fled
Assert thy boasted empire o'er the Dead.
Call forth the ashes that so long have lain
Within thy tombs and bid them live again!"

Thus Claudio ;—then, as in our dreams we see
Strange changes with no link of sense, so he
Through fevered medium sees a fiery glow
Thrill through the heavens and the plain below,
Gleam with a brazen light!   The sultry air
Against his parched lips burns, and lurid glare
Flashed from the lightnings conjured in his brain,
Blears every sense excepting that of pain.
"Water! I thirst!   Did heav'n send rain to lie
For nought upon the ground but mockery?
I feel no moisture on the sod—a flame
Seems stealing from it!   In the Virgin's name
Give water quickly! or I die!
                              Oh! Heaven!—
A flowing stream unto my prayer is given!
I feel the large drops fall upon my hand!"

It is his life-blood dripping to the sand !
Wildly he seeks the welling stream and sips
The sanguine current with his eager lips—
Then fainter than before renews the cry ;
"Water!   Bring water quickly—or I die !"

As midst Sahara's wastes a spring unseen,
Though miles of scorching desert intervene,
Sends subtle freshness that a great despair
Alone detects upon the sun-dried air,
E'en thus to him an influence undefined
Brings instinct of relief.
                              The evening wind
Thrills the seared olive leaves, and shades of
      night,
Steal from the hills the fallen gems of light,
When 'tween the soldier and the sunset sky,
A woman clad in ash-hued drapery,
With bowed head shrouded in a gleaming
      hood,
That marks her one of Mercy's sisterhood,
Stands—with a goblet filled up to the brim,
Tending the limpid life-draught down to him.

Impetuously he grasps the cup—when lo !
Arrested by a murmur'd " Claudio,"
He starts—his eyes strain through the dusk and
    trace
A look they know upon the woman's face.

" Melina !—Hence ! away !   Bring not to me
The life thou owest to *her !*   Tend not to me
Hands haunted by *her* woe !   The saints on
    high
Shall end, in pitying love, this agony—
Not thou !"

        Then he his yearning lip restrains
And flings the cup untasted to the plains,
Whilst as the goblet broken quits his hand
He falls back dead upon the crimsoned sand.

    *   *   *   *   *   *

The Night comes upward from the East and
    stands
To mourn and shroud the Dead.
                        Her shadowy hands

For flowers spread wreaths of stars, and from
    her tears
Spring mists that rise and fall.
                        Through countless years
Thus has—thus shall—she come, to fold away
Beneath her silver wings, the Hopes of Day.

Swift & Co., 55, King Street, Regent Street, W.